AF342357

UNEARTHED

Janet Marie Rogers

Unearthed

leaf press

Library and Archives Canada Cataloguing in Publication

Rogers, Janet Marie, 1963-
    Unearthed / Janet Marie Rogers.

Poems.
ISBN 978-1-926655-33-8

    I. Title.

PS8585.O395198U54 2011   C811'.6   C2011-905520-1

Cover Image: *Not of this Earth* © Lee Claremont www.leeclaremont.ca.
Janet Rogers original photo by Mike Lacroix
Editor: Garry Gottfriedson.
Clouds Background © Moophoto | Dreamstime.com

We gratefully acknowledge the support of the Canada Council for the Arts and the British Columbia Arts Council.

PRINTED IN CANADA on FSC certified papers.

Leaf Press
Box 416
Lantzville, B.C., Canada
V0R 2H0
www.leafpress.ca

This collection is dedicated to the memory
of my niece Chayah (1980–2011).
She left us at the young age of 30.
Some souls are too sensitive for this world
and too stubborn to stay. We wish her a blessed
spirit journey, until we see her again.

Table of Contents

IDENTITY

LOVE

When We Were Stars

I used to be homeless
you were too
no land, no politics
oxygenless astronauts
galaxies without parameters
lucky stars waiting for wishes

we used to gaze upon the globe
and you'd say "looks like suspended marbled water"
I liked the light and shadow
the way the bowl transformed to a cup
then a knife and back again

the other stars
made lightening trails
blazing past us
to their end

"let them go" we'd sing
without dominion for our souls
it was all so simple
then I fell
and you did too

landing in very different territories
miles away from each other
and the politics between us
only grew

Before the Next Life

I never see
my donations resurface
in the thrift store
where do they go?
it seems they pass through
a purgatory of sorts
not ready to reincarnate
for someone else, as something else
somewhere down the road

it was a cloudless Saturday
in another city
when you gifted me
with turquoise
said it was to honour
all I did for you

looking back now
I earned every bead
and deserved thousands more

you owe me

we stood on the edge
the naked cliff under us
looking out over a characterless sea
small sailboats floated by
slow and matter-of-factly
made me think about ships of bounty
and if these were mine
I thought they'd be bigger
I felt a pang of disappointment
like an inheritance coming in
jaw-droppingly lower than expected

in a fit of remembrance
I gather the blue beads,
stuff them inside
a fake velvet bag

and take to the streets at night
a racoon in reverse
leave them at the back door
of the thrift store
as objects of rejection
before their next life

Colossal Discoveries

spirit come back to me
help me
navigate safely
return   and be   a part
of me

inside you ride
like waves hitting shore
rising   receding   swelling

end   lesslee
          end   lesslee
                    end   lesslee

          disconnected

patiently waiting…
connections are taking time
and the moon continues
to move in her cycles
opening and closing
the curtains

PEEK-A-BOOH

in this moment
a thousand realities collide
the road is still there
the ocean   keeps beating
the cows   are still killed
and we   keep eating

end-lessly
end-lessly
end-lessly

          moving
along-side-each-other's   reality

the beauty of this world lures us
we move towards it
relating to places
where earth's body stops and liquid prairies flow

we know

the closer we are
the closer we'll be
this is time's constant
now and forever more

and less lies and less lies and less lies and

we conquer vast sands
feel god's breath
like mist on our skin
lick salty spice
from our lips
burn this moment into memory
new reality
taking shape
like embryos of thought

in this moment

dreams repeating

nightmares

feelings

Free to Love

I am free

open heart

wounded and all

my love is honest

come what may

it is clear skies after rain

I am the rain

passion

should not be confused

with romance

although it lives

in the same neighbourhood

we are the train, we are words, we feel pain

and make medicine

The Great Mystery does not inspire questions

but holds answers

it's awful

where love lives,

there are ten more loves to come

it is not for the faint of heart

but weakens doubt and dismay

I am an empty cup, sometimes two

I am free

to love, too

Distractions

the stars are distracting me
with their beauty
keeping me from duty
and purpose

your voice is distracting me
telling me to move on
don't linger too long
where visions are born
cities get torn
between progress and politics

nations balance, they straddle
two worlds
choose sides out of doubt
or compliance
exercise caution
in our need to proceed
along new paths
where we feel our way
into dark tomorrows
moving with ancient faith
we create deep tracks
for anthropologists
to make fiction of our past

where are you now?

where are we now?

even on the outside
we still hold a place
embrace liberation
inside, living on the outside
of normal

ground-zero
where concepts of minority
are actually the majority
and all of us who don't fit in

begin to win votes
undo, what we know
not to be true
live by our own codes
love those we want
and only those who love us
back

Descendant

angel
touch your wings
so lightly to earth
feel the magnetic
pull that keeps me here

angel
understand
my love affair with land
extends beyond flesh
generations and creation
my love affair began
when I was like you
an anchorless entity
weightless spirit
devolved from solids
only to serve those
below

angel
touch the ground once
you'll want more
you'll know home
and want to stay
trade your wings for feet
plant them firmly on earth
and tell me not if
but how long
you've wanted this

angel
cease to fly
and sit by me at the fire
here you will confidently confess
disappointments of heaven
the endless thankless acts
like prison chains ready
to be cast off
forever

rest angel
let the good shepherd tend to his flock
rest your weary wings
tell me everything
come down angel
to me

Many Things Greater

my skin is too heavy
it needs to be shed
I take what is good
inside the earth
soak my bones in mud packs
lie inside healing springs
and dissolve
all
emotional trauma
unresolved problems
leaving me numb
I want to crawl inside
the Mother and listen
to disembodied voices
learn their wisdom
know my choices
and act on them

MY song is sung
soothing and strong
the sounds of sorrow
collide to make symphonies
sympathy sounding resounding out

what happened to love?
where is honour and support?
when did men begin to believe
women are disposable?

quarterly reports announce recessions
I played the fool too many times
we all reach that certain age when
brave understanding wins
and we spend the days
mending fences
repairing defences
focusing on how to detect lies

where are the miracles?
I expected them
these princess steps
lead to queen
I follow   never to know
LOVE
and honour

the greatest fears are illusions
turned inward that grow
as cancerous answers
questions I may
take to the grave
would rather fly than fight
but this skin weighs me down

many things greater
I deserve
I deserve
…greater things

Physical Reflections

It was on the beaten path
where we travelled last
both struggling
victory unsure
each step deliberate
until you turned away

continuity of reality
creates truth
and routine reinforces our faith
it was done in a moment
of honour and grace
when I left the ring
the silver one with the garnet
atop the rock where we stopped
and took in the liquid pacific

there was a feather
a gift from vulture
we followed his flight
and remembered the forces
that brought us together
the way you used my affections
and want of connection
to get your way, to be entertained
the bird gift I kept and gave
the rest away

warm spring winds
kiss prairie grasses
and all is well again
April rain descends
like ghosts visiting
deepening the meaning
of regifting, recycling
feeding the mother
what she needs

humanity's answers are heard
in the beating
of wet drops against
wood-smoke-warmed dens

the place between cruel altitudes
and marshy mountain feet
is Goldilocks Land
midway, ready, waiting
host to troubled souls passing
inhabiting canyons, healing
needing rich solitude in soil
the swirling ions
mixed with vegetation
cannot be duplicated
become a drug to those
who know the power

I am not a tourist
NYC is me and my people
we started and continued to build
after the Dutch, after Ellis Island immigrants
after Wall Street goblins took it over
the rock beneath the sidewalk
beneath my shoes
beneath my soul
carried familiar energy
welcomed me home
informing my every step
ancestral GPS directed me back

we are not alone
in our loneliness
many similar souls
walk on borrowed ground
we are all connected
to the earth's heart
and our own
a symbiotic balance of
physical, spiritual, emotional

persons passing through
we cannot leave it, it loves us too

mid-summer season
beach rocks warm
spread medicinal heat

I shape my back to fit the curves
there is no pain
only sounds of lazy waves
massaging sands
send me, I'm gone
inside
escape
meditate
reattached to land
together floating on oceans
riding the turtle's back
realizing our relation to astronomy
the galaxy scribing poetry
in stars
we are not far
we are close
we are the same
I am the rock and water
I am the sand and stars
the reflections are endless
continuous
simple math cannot express it
but it is something we are born knowing, so know it

growing still are my affections for you
I lose nothing in this confession
but free the words, free my spirit
in the pure truth of them
feel, rather than know
my intentions meant to reach you
wherever your spirit has travelled
perhaps our paths will cross again
our hearts will call each other home

a home, a house
the curious experience where
trees stood witness
to the biological combining of hearts
the love that was birthed
we feed the earth
and grow crops from it
feel it in the rain drops
that bless our faces fused with tears of acceptance
fearing nothing that survives us
love lives here

It Can Happen

I'd rather be the tree
than the swinging fruit
everything
looks like water
through the eyes
of passion
inside a dream
inside yourself
there are things
that want to be written
and there are things
that want to be said
I am neither
the tree nor the fruit
but the dirt
from which they both grow
I am the sun
and sometimes the rain
passion you see in me
is a reflection
of your own, so sing
long wide sounds
sing your joy
I miss the music
without you
the notes inside the flute
stay silent
I am forced
to make my own
from thin air
there is no warm inspiration
just the sun
important words get tossed
ping-pong like
there are things
that can be taught
and there are things
we just learn
I am not your teacher
I am a poet
with words and the dirt
beneath them

Conflicted Loyalties

I have learned to live
with conflicted loyalties
like child
asked to keep secrets
and told
to tell lies

I have learned
not to trust the water
but to climb heights
and let myself fall

we are dancing strange dances
with words and looks
and the music no longer
makes sense or pleases me

my thoughts are raw
and real
too real for my spirituality
yet too naïve for my prayers

I don't wear feathers
to please you
and I have not learned to clean fish
or keep silent

I know that love has a price
and I'll pay, whatever the cost
to love and keep loving
my skin, my imperfect people

I miss the language I never had
am loyal to the idea of it
no stone can break us up
not a bulldozer
or cannonball

Arrival

after the flood
wet impressions
evaporated memory lessons
of what once was
fires waiting
for words burning
bring your letters of love
set it aflame
fertilize the path with ash
make way for new love
coming in spring
some other spring
and "home" no longer holds the same
comfort
it once did

I am falling
down the rabbit hole
shrinking, expanding
constantly adapting
it is my magic medicine
it is all I know
even the ambitious buds grow impatient
they want to be big too

eagles know how to be humble
and crows can change anytime they want
my arm used to be a tree
now it is a branch
with it, I reach up to the sky
and pull down remembrances
left from last time
people can never be
illegal or illegitimate
the earth knows this
we make trade for space
our time for this place
my confetti canon is aimed
in your direction
Ta-Dah – in Tonto-speak
means I have arrived

Drift

believe me it was easy
seeing you drift from body to spirit
to a place
knowing   I needn't follow
watching you float
above yourself
making a gentle ascension
shift-shaping   leaving one world

you left
and I understood
a knowing that lives on
inside, as solid as bone
time became my ally
and free will, a friend
feeling you venture forward
finding your way in the end

you let go so did I

I was not left alone
bits that connected us
keep me company
and visit me throughout the day
every time I hear that song
and in rare moments of peace

in your absence
I walk on the road
knowing you join
for a block or two
it is my custom
to feed you – though
your body won't receive
at times ask you to leave
when I feel you've stayed
too long

drift

be gone

it's what I'd do…

Climb the Tunnel

"wait, don't leave me"
then laughter
he knew what I was doing
a rolled-up picture of a dancer
sits in the middle of the hollow
of a tree
four years over
time to really (let) go

climbing the tunnel with purpose
bits of him close to the sun
outside in the elements

his letters would go elsewhere
the river perhaps
if they don't get caught in ice jams
the letters left suspended in a time
when I was blind and could only see
he was not with me

he called me a "gift from Creator"
used all kinds of that language
found in new age healing spiritual
circle – colour – ritual – medicine stuff
he spoke of "good red roads,
and long hours in the lodge"
feeling the grass dancer inside him
come alive

I dreamt of many coffins
littering hillsides
falling overlapping others
so many believing in healing
his healing was troubled
from the start

the final dance with his devil
ended on a high note

complete understanding surprised even me
four years…so how is the air up there
free to dance with ravens
and sing your songs with the wind
tell us from your new perch

how is the air up there?

Desperate Crazy Christmas Love Poem

frost bites my nose
chill-filled winds bitch-slap my cheeks
loss of sensation in the toes
one more block – then home

three a.m. your call rang me awake
in half-dream state you explained
"there is nothing here for me, I'm going back home"
could have been a number of desperate souls
calling on christmas eve
it was you – the reason I uprooted
and left sixty percent of what I owned behind
to be here – with you

even in the beginning
there were challenges

I thought we'd endure
time has a funny way of showing you truth
with patience and silence
it waits out our weaknesses

we keep mistaking each other's kindness for love
but now in a season when congeniality is everywhere
I see acts of manners
are nothing to construct a relationship from

on go the boots
to aid you in your desperate hours
feed you encouraging words
let you seduce me into bed
leave silently, shaking my head

this is my gift to you
my constant unconditional vow
to be there for you
and like the saints who listen to your prayers
I ask for nothing in return
but take what you provide for me
connection, kindness
and completion

Crow Hop

there is new blood
inside me now
stirred up potions
upset, upside down
make promises
and do the opposite
I've come to expect this
I feel sick
my heart is racing
tides rise and rise
tensions build
inspirations explode
don't pretend
with me
we both know
it's okay
we know

just don't forget
that's all I ask
don't forget
what we did
how we did it
and why

I am satisfied
knowing from this time
we have history
curious
and unkind

goodbye
goodbye

Amalga-Mates

they came together
after the rains
robins within the city
waiting, delaying
a union fated in the stars
inside the Scorpio/Leo dance
spun magic and medicines
creation 1 and creation 2
filtered through
six years apart, they are taught
to wait, as Mama bird learned
nothing comes until you wait
and are ready
and gut-timing tells you
amalgamate, connect the forces
swirling as spring winds
carrying answers in on
circling fringes, marrying everything
a universal wedding connecting people and resources
overwhelming natural forces
by choice and skill

Lady Red Breast waits and watches
her soul mate become crusty
stays out of his way
expecting nothing more, avoiding disappointment
the constant project grows and serves the goal
while she takes flight
to find food, build a house for the muse
a place of honour where she paints
with expert plumes a future
picture from instinct faith and pain

POLITICS

What the Carver Knows

he sits on sidewalks
sizing up passers-by
clutching his curved knife
drawing deep confident gouges
transforming yellow cedar

"bear?" he's asked
"beaver" he explains
and waits for change
we all wait for change
says, he's been to church, yesterday
they pray for him there
"worth more than money
thank god it stopped raining"

two bucks, he thinks, is a lot
drinks decaf between wood shavings
red pride has not abandoned him
resides inside, quiet like heartfelt memories
a childhood, good and cared for
a family strong and revered
he is here

he claims the cement as home
on a damp street corner
in a city which sees so many like him
it rolls its eyes as numbers grow
he moans and bleeds
lets droplets fall
onto a thirsty earth
seeping down to meet
the bones of those who've gone before

we live envious
of his skills and ability to survive
while we complain daily
of superficial hardships
and spoiled-rotten heartaches

the beaver bites back
the carver smiles sideways
the rain begins again
while we run for cover

Just Watch

you will see them
along the horizon
watch
let them pass
ghostlike
silent as gossamer light
catching your eye
at sunset

they rest during the day
staying away
making magic
taking shape

you will see them
tracing soft earth
connecting to the universe
casting spells where workers dwell
holding it all together

they speak to us
and tell of a time
yet to be
they see what sits far
on horizons and make clear
our visions, where reality is conceived
we see the portals
other planes untouched by us

they are mountain movers
carvers of rivers
ground shakers
and wind symphonies

MOQW/MOQW?ESPEYE?WIXT

when it began
it didn't begin
as work
but birthrights
responsibilities
stewardships
a kind of vigilance
in leadership

the governments call
stubborn misunderstanding
theatrical stages set
for round-table stand-offs

it began
when provincial treaties
soaked Indigenous title
like water bombs
over wildfires
which never quite
saw the light of day
lying at the foot of the
Indian Summit

unification
through common discrimination
surviving under one umbrella
touting slogans saying
"together we stand divided we perish"

boardroom battlefields birthed leaders
charged with the dissection of their own nations
control of national constipation/constitution
(con)promising "S"overeign policies
"more please"
The "S" word
we know is rooted in
colonials doling out
one for you, five for me
turning our people into well-dressed beggars

perhaps it was
the adoption of the newcomers'
processes, possessions
walking away from our ways
(listen to the women)
even the little home-makers
scared 'em

or the unprecedented necessity
to work within unfamiliar warfare/welfare
with no way to measure success
or knowing when it all ends

how far have we really come
ladies and gentlemen?

gathered as a valiant brown union
miraculous agreements
formed the most basic of agendas
decided in a time before
we were all called "Aboriginal"
set out to improve
social and economic truths
and today we fight the same
DFO that continues to commit
old crimes from four decades ago

In 1975
the goal was
to increase the life expectancy
of our people
to learn the steps of the land
claim dance
and put into legalese
words that allowed
Indians to be Indians

What country *IS* this?

are we in some far-fetched
futuristic sci-fi
or drunken spaghetti western?

this history reads like
badly written fiction
Steven Spielberg
wouldn't even believe it
James Cameron maybe
the new white messiah
story-stealing ally
but that's an aside…

lets look at the players
Indian Affairs cast
ex-RCMP and ex-army
in the role of bully antagonist

Oscar worthy acting…or is it?

The Indians' motivations
swing from protector to justifier
and mental shape-shifter
mind-wizards tying to make
governments understand

at no time throughout
the script do we hear
the protagonists recite
their lines together
however the same lines
are recited in the remake
some fifteen years later

we survived the work
the artificial divisions
the brown bureaucracy
and even hired white pens
to write our own
recipes of defence

we learned the language
embraced paper and legislation
to get our way by any means
we maintain
reclaim
mountains
the seas
the complex combinations
of desert and marsh
and blizzard-ravaged northlands

this land *they* call
British
we know
we own

the original names
are never forgotten

they call it what they want
we know it by another

Bold?

no – more brass

bold suggests
something born
of courage

no

this
is born
of something offensive

like being stuck
on a five-hour flight
going east
to a city
you hate
sat beside
someone
with stink feet
but you're canadian
so you say nothing

brassy
and
begging
to be responded to
it's me confronting you
in the middle
of a downtown street
about
rent
overdue
and your reply
is
bold
not courageous-bold
but ignorant-bold
indignant-bold
because
you are
canadian

Reclamation

young ones are angry
women rally
a community is tired of trying
to make space
and keep territories safe

humans push back time
over population spilling
into tricky treaties
un-honoured, ripped and torn

how do we articulate
multi-generational hate
and calm our restless spirits?

they say "stand and fight
a good fight
use all the tools left"
we are blessed
with good minds
our choices are wise

today we fight
as a last resort
when request after request
goes ignored

we take a stand based
on inherent land claims
we are finished waiting
for your good faith
to kick in
...so it begins

young warriors pierce the soil
with the pole of our flag
find inspiration around the fire
where we gather as clans
and sing our songs
a call to arms

young ones are angry
and women rally

Peace, Truth, Reconciliation and Cold Porridge

I am choking on lessons, cut hair and bloody
bended knees. Money-measured apologies paid
for pain and suffering. Only the colonials boil
it down to dollars and sensibility. No humility,
humanity I understand, you're just trying to make
your god happy.

—words, war, words, war, words, were, words,
    war, words, where, words, were, words

—curator, creator, curator, creator, curator, crater,
    creator, greater, crater, curator, creator

—anthropology, apology, anthropology, apology,
    apathy, a party, anthropology, apology

—indian affairs, indians fair, indian affairs, indians
    fair, indie fear, indian affairs, indians

I am NOT aboriginal. I am not your fool. I make
the books, you can read them. I choose my titles, so
don't tell me, don't police me. From this moment
on, now and forever more, it will be undone. I am
laughing big gut hurting cheek bursting hilarious
laughing. Fuck!

—contract, contact, contract, contact, con-act,
    contract, contact, call back, contract, contact

—beyond, belong, beyond, belong, be gone, begin,
    beyond, belong, beg, beyond, be gone

—police, please, police, please, politics, pollutes,
    please, police, politics, police, please

—living, leaving, laughing, loving, longing,
    leaving, living, luring, longing, living, leaving

We can never host enough fundraising dinners,
wash whitie's cars and pass the blanket dances

to raise enough money for plane tickets to see the
pope, buy new clothes to kiss his filthy ring. My
legs can never be strong enough to hold me long
enough to stand in line for the cavity search before
entering G-chambers to ask Harper, "What will
YOU do, for US?"

—gnaw at us, not us, gnaw at us, not us, none of
   us, no guts, not tell us, gnaw at us, not us

—indian, in and in, indian, in and in, indian,
   indetermine, in and in, indian, in and in and in

—legitimate, litigate, legitimate, litigate, alienate,
   all hate, legitimate, litigate, alienate, hate

—arrogance, error against, arrogance, error against,
   air or gain, arrogance, error against

Hold me back, no more. We are born with freedom
through activism and learn all too soon how to
build blockades around our own successes. We
may have forgotten how to live. We love our
booze. We want to buy things. The secret need to
breed the Indian out of us almost worked.

—activist, acting nice, activist, acting nice,
   acquiesce, activist, acting nice, activist, acting

—optimist, opportunist, optimist, opportunist,
   operate, optimist, O.P.P., opportunist

—branded, brain-dead, branded, brain-dead,
   branded, brunette, bandit, branded, brunette

—confederate, counterfeit, confederate, counterfeit,
   conference, confess, confederate

I live by the wampum law. They paddle one canoe,
we'll paddle our canoe, and maybe we'll see you at
the end of the river. I have never been consulted on
all the Indian laws I'm made to live by. My father's

vote never made headlines and the grand chief
only extends a hand to his friends. Not me.

—direct, derelict, delicate, direct, derelict, delicate,
  direct, derelict, delicate, dick, derelict

—contagious, contact us, contagious, control us,
  correct count, contagious, control us

—survival, serve all, survival, serve all, severe fall,
  serve all, survival, suicide fall

—pedophile, petrified, pedophile petrified,
  pedophile, personified, petrified, pedophile

There is no arguing that even after the pay off,
the apology and the many offices designated to
deal with the Indian problem, we still experience
Canada's polite form of racism, back-handed
compliments and, "Oh, thanks for the body bags
and slop buckets." And really, I just wish people
would stop writing about us like recipes trying to
define the ingredients, the complex combinations
of spirit, intelligence, wit and strength.

—calories, calm ease, calories, calm ease, color
  ease, calm ease, calories, color ease

—new religion, new regions, new religion, new
  regions, new reasons, regeneration, religion

—story share, soft ware, story share, song share,
  tell and show, talent show, borrow

—residential, residual, residential, residual,
  reciprocal, residual, reschedule, responsible

The words birthed from the back of my tongue.
I want them to bounce from my lips, exorcised
like the demon language dug from deep guttural
places undetected by X-ray and close examination.
Everybody can't be dead already. I want my
words back!

Yet to Be

the face of my friend
reflected in archival men
staring blankly into camera lens

what purpose would it serve
to preserve their stance on film?

he knew he was here
left plenty of evidence in flesh
descendants and friends

the origins of this man
sit high atop his feathered head
inside barren mountains and the river's bend
in a look that says
"catch me if you can"

long lives live as files
kept tight behind metal
blood of my kind, a mirror
staring into itself reflecting back and back
while we drown in waves of responsibility

who can we be?

that would make them smile from the grave
let them rest in peace while we practise
what they preached

the autumn of our knowing is yet to be…

their magic makes so much from thin air
personal tides   restore pride
the chord attaching me to you is long and elastic
and can not be broken
by years of lies or silence
we bring our memories together

ancestors share tea and time
gossip about our trials
and weak triumphs
and discuss
what is yet to be

Smack

I was just being myself
no one else
didn't know
there'd be a show down
between the new girl in town
and the nasty pale-skinned Indian

told to dial down
the mohawk
play down the shine
leave a little thunder
behind for them

not today, or tomorrow

to this day
I hold myself up
stand as an example
dedicated to the purpose
of place
and if you don't like it
well…

rhythm word verses

reverse trauma
insecure drama
I am Osama flying your planes
using your blame
crumbling your hate
with the same

I gave it time
and proved
that I am untouchable
incredible
indestructible
wonderful

as revenge I seduce your men
and leave them
broken-hearted, ineffective
unable to love another

my paper membership
puts me in territory of Salish
I have been cut
that's my blood
that stains your land
and flows thick in the rivers,
feeds the fish you feed
your children

how does it taste?

I taste victory
and stand on this land
take over the airwaves
and sing my songs
inside your house
where protocol requires you to listen

I never heard it
but I heard it
"go home"
and I never said it
but I said it
"get used to it"
that's the sound
of my heels
digging in deep not that I needed
to prove it but I proved it
facts are facts and bullshit
fades away, look
get an eyeful
try not to go blind
from my light!

Insult to Injury

racism
colonialism
christie blatchford journalism
does not fail
to drive the last nail
of insult into the graves
of pickton's victims
by calling them
drug addicts
accurate?
or sensationalist?
she, herself, stands
on the corner
not bothering to
venture further down
the colonial
road for reasons
that got them
there

she does her part
to feed the beast
scraps straight
out of context
absent of details
with this stone
she kills not one
bird, but two

murderer

who cares?
not the soft pudding premier
who makes half promises
in time to set public inquiries

perhaps another apology
is on the way
post election apathy

these crimes
have rooted themselves
in seven generations to come
look to the horizon
this country
has a fascination
with the Indigenous
not one of respect
but like a grand experiment
testing our limits
we are rats
identities stretched
while they look for signs and prizes
of who we are and who we are to be

she
writes us up
nineteen dollars a word
borrowing from
the usual cache
stereotypical
burdens of the nation
and pickton
just another
sick immigrant
benefiting from
the racist justice
journalist
canadians
enjoying their
canadian lives

Love Your Country

do I offend you?

your sensitivity
is not my responsibility

listen to me
my expression and personal politics
dampen your fantasies of me
keep listening

that's my ancestors' voice
in your ears
speaking clearer than clear
you know it
in your colonial bones

my hair is black
skin brown
and I don't apologize
if you're sick
of hearing about us

I see you are smart
I see you sit silently
digesting your hate
hoping to avoid
the label "racist"

well racist
conventional characteristics
fit the corporate profile
smile, and flash your passport
congratulations, you make the cut

Through the Eye of a Needle

this day holds the potential of a matchstick
salty, ready to strike, burn bright
consume by fire leaving charred destruction
in its path

boozy smoke fills the air
catching thick vernaculars
cascading downwards to crowds
badly dressed blue collars, together
find comfort in collective simpleness
reproducing mediocrity

dry-skinned elders give up
sit back, cross their arms
to the wanton masses demanding answers
feeling squeezed to the limit
they reply "find it on the internet"

bonus rounds
promise new cars, free education, healing
foundations
massive distractions while crows steal
seeds planted in shallow beds
yielding half-sized vegetation
enough to feed one-third

hear the beaver's tail slap hard
inducing pools of truth
to cautiously wade through

this is the future we've been waiting for

Are You Listening?

why talk about territory
why vote or go to war
I make   no threat

I take it outside

culture claims   indifference
inside language talk
with rented words from the future

I cannot deny
the energy/matter
person I am
the people I come from
the way we live

time & land are unrelated
what do you hear
inside my sound combinations
flat notes, float, sink
meaningless vocables
chants, take a chant
mysteries repeating
history swallowed
singers keeping
sound combinations
I am singing
constantly singing

just remember…
awake-ness is not the same
as awareness
I could care less
when asked how you fit in
through impatience I embrace
accelerated methods of communication

imbalanced sustainability
there is not enough land
to grow all the food
needed to feed all of us

some of us have got to go
at least stop feeding people
into the problem

come-you
com-pute
ca-peeshe
ka-pow

intelligence is a trickster transforming
looking like a prince
with solutions
given time is revealed to be
a northern beggar
mixed race rutter-less brother rudder
culture-less court jester

drums are sounding
the women are coming
and we're not asking
we're telling
our place on the land
is in front
on our feet   leading
our time is now

Come to Mama, baby!

time and land face
opposite directions
looking backward to the west
where everything is sung
into being
we – are born from song
keep singing
keep breathing: the melodies
that made you

"I am" bringing
ways of my land
to your liquid threshold
hold on – let go
go east – keep going east
get well – sigh-a-narrah

I Am Singing, Of Tomorrow –
I Am Singing, Of Love

of land, of love of land

Rightful Place

it begins
with the *word*
this begets the sound
birthing the song
honouring the earth

it begins
with the *call*
to create
fabricate
with gifts
you are blessed
make the best
the boldest
the most honest
of offerings
to pass on…

it begins with a *step*

and then the next

until suddenly, you are in the middle of a journey
you never intended to take, leading you to deep
places inside yourself, rapidly transporting
beyond flesh and reason to the truest you

…are we there yet

it begins
inside your skin
growing slowly
like blossoms
in spring
taking their awakening
and rightful place
as do you

it begins
with a *dream*   dreamt over and over again

something you can't
comprehend
but holds you
like food
in the stomach
digesting

trusting

bursting

releasing

It begins…

the word

    the call

        the step

           the skin

               the dream

                   the word

                       the word

                           the word

Inconvenient Answers

a lone shoe sits on a highway pointing north
human freeways flow
fleeing floods and natural disasters
they came to replicate ancestral journeys
authentically perpetuate protocols and permissions
open gates do not discriminate
nature does not judge Skin, Sex, Faith
and does not count our money
uprooted, like saplings by hand
displaced addresses lost
razor wire lined trenches
protect destruction
tragedy makes pasty ghosts weep
and the Indians say, "We knew it."
privileged parliaments demand presidential responses
lines go dead and days pile up
like unclaimed bodies left along river banks
plywood rafts provide the escape
the light of this darkness comes in opportunities to rebuild
set aside differences, judgements, work the tools together
let's share a vision and just plain work that shit out
take the complaints and turn them into action
actions to motivate others
then we will know "God helps those, who help themselves."
and those who help themselves are powerful
and a whole bunch of us make unstoppable nations
for the people – by the people, where's the politics in that
we will not need to see I.D.
we will know you just by looking at you
and look what happens, when that happens, connections
honest trades and exchanges of skills
take a minute to see it – can you see it now believe it
we are better, more worse than we think
I can be kinder, more cruel than expected
the future is brighter, more bleak
my people pass like pendulums on a swing of hope?
exercising lazy faith, allowing it to live a brief life
abandoned before the miracles are born?
this is the grand marathon of chance
steady on brothers and sisters
steady on
we'll be fine

The Last Frontier

wakeful imagination
activation
the last frontier
two parts half-truths
one part vision

spirit vs. science
habitual rituals
nonsense and empty
actions challenge the logical
learn to un-learn

forced voices push
into consciousness
teachers teaching
one lesson at a time
broken stories
find their way
back into places
near extinction

the last frontier
survival skills
spirits say
this isn't make believe
this is real

distance
means nothing
urban disease
means nothing
explorations
in insomnia
take you to lonely streets
following faint footprints
walking, waking
until finally, you are there

the very last frontier

Hurricane Rage

inside black tunnels
darkness strange takes up space
covers like icky summer
sweat sweat

compasses
moved by passions
and righteous anger
rage has a place
survive survive

I sit with my silly fit
feel it gnaw away at my guts
twist my head around
as I dig my heels deeper
into my itty bit of earth
leave my mark
remember remember

"I was here, mutha-fuka"

put that on a flag
and wave it in your face
and I walk back
into my collective reality
precious creative rage
delicious dessert
using tasty stanzas
choke choke

some may grow
but we will all
shit it out in the end
ain't it true
that's what's same
between me and you
we waste
time time

ego driven endeavours

I know this and use it
sell my/self short
bring my thirst
to dirty rivers
I feel
cheap cheap
I have choice
I have routine
I have lessons
I have the familiar
I have intelligence ?
          but I have television intelligence

(R)age, we don't have to wait for

Perspective

water/spirits/share
ancient questions
answers – connections
finally made

Red-Black-Grey live
in generous mysterious
ways
a place to bathe
and   let   go

Grey-Yellow-White
forged signatures
commitments
never to be
nature takes
its course

our future   floats

promises/turned/tricks
wheels spin one more rotation
witnesses cheer on natiONs
bravery is rarely exercised
generations won't rebel

the spell is bro-ken
it's all   sooooo   goooood

White-Brown-Black
foot paths
beneath layers
of yester-years
destroyed/reborn
as something else
retold
to fit
the times

daily radiation...

thickens extinction
quickens
and we lose ways
to say what we mean

all the lands
have been tamed
and for this, we pay

it takes vigilance
and violent resistance
to sustain the minuscule offerings
under our feet

sounds like complaints
but try it on – this truth
maybe it fits you too

the snow has slowed
only this year it fell in spring
when the earth should be
sweating vegetation and preparing
for searing heat
gradual and natural

we can fly
like migrating birds
but even the birds
have lost their way
instead they remain on foreign shores
convene on beaches with deceased whales
and immature fruit from flooded crops
that come to your table
at triple the price

what is wild is real
I fear the sky may be the last frontier
the higher we go
the more insult we pay

to those who truly belong
let your grass grow long
light a fire on the sand
be glad you knew it
before it became strange

IDENTITY

Drunken Shaman

he's like
any other drunk
on the street, broken teeth
grease
sits heavy in his hair
from last week

he does his best
to lure you close
in gravel-voiced compliments
he says   he knows you
he says   he likes your shoes
he begs for attention
to be taken
at face value
feeling the sidewalk
shift from under him

brown wing-ed angels
perch on either shoulder
one singing
Tina Turner's version of
I Wanna Take You Higher
the other pounding out
pow wow rhythms
with his talk
a beat that never leaves him

he holds court
and tells fortunes
to his cronies
seducing them with tales
of robbery, prejudice and bullshit
stolen stories, wishing they were his
every now and then, speaking truth
so raw and real, it leaves them silent
for weeks

each night he greets
the blue clad lads

offering to escort him home
his magic does not work on them
entire cities can be erected
in the gaps of their misunderstanding
drunken shaman
is not a victim
he chose to be
the visual reminder
of our delicate successes
teaches us what not to teach
the children
and he survives
a life
many of us
could not

every day
working his medicine
left to him by trappers
dancers and traders
a family who watches over him
while the shaman receives his visions

Change-Makers

Pacific hearts split
like separating cells
grow and divide
fulfilling unspoken
purposes to find
themselves and home

North, South love
covers unseen expanses
flesh and land-blood
lives defined with
intelligent politics
cultural and lawful
born on the very territories
that shape civil societies

our connected oceans
carry pacific passengers
along liquid horizons
Change-Makers coming
bringing messages of collective integrity
based in respectful progress
the way it was meant to be
before immigration
written in words

young leaders
look to their elders
with split-heart questions
knowing traditions live in more
than one realm
sung in harmonies
overlapping memories
blending and sending
positive waves washing back
three lifetimes away

our warm homelands
gifted to us to keep
like promises in the belly

there is no telling
how far the line goes
but we know we come
from difference
and distance travelling
on parallel paths
collective actions
tell of challenges
overcome with solidarity
and resolve
using education and technology
as tools
connecting like-minds
words resonating waves
on rocks
repeating our walk
one generation to the next

spirit makes it all possible
we carry on as proud people
spinning so much love
from one split heart

Mountain Passage

flawless horizons
shrink behind smudgy skies
wave good-bye to prairie-kin
dusty-skinned
brown proud families

challenging roads
leading west
hold tight the reins
of a horse
taking the course
one hour
to the next

cowboy towns
leak secrets
crumbling
between loose bricks
exposing ugly insides

I pass through
as pioneer
never been here
western doors open
wait for my return
travel in silence
while mountain spirits guide
and usher me through
slowing my motions
in an asphalt trance

unkind roads
host decorated shoulders
crosses and flowers
another hour passes
reflection takes hold

I sit in the middle
of a movie
passing all around
staying the course
breaking ground
riding all the way
home

Highway 80 East

it wasn't legend

it was human ego

that separated

the sky from the earth

knowing the living

would need a margin

at least that wide

and forever widening

the sky twists itself down

to take a reckless touch

wanting reconnecting

random receding

only liquid earth

lava dirt can coil itself

downward

stack and overlap

before blasting clear

with all those signs

for firework sales

don't they know it's all

gonna blow anyway?

no purchase necessary

let the truckers take

the night shift even though they

regret the black asphalt

for keeping them slaves

nuthin but direction all round them

and going nowhere fast

what are we all haul'n?

open roads like open sores begin

to leak secrets, confessions

left like roadkill

turn into dust storms to rain back down

as white memories

the elderly envy

those roads for the honesty

it took them a lifetime to learn

black birds fly in twos

circling pale herds blended against

golden spring grasses

not a river or a lake

to break the monotony

barely anything

of distraction only freedom

and too much of that

creates confusion

Fear and Laughing

demons defying description
drunk on privilege
and Jack Daniels
thick-blooded residents
resist laws of the land
they have no business
being on
sand traps and landscapes
wide open and
virgin-like

romantic soundtracks
paying unwanted visits
you never intended to
tune them in

permission to enter
comes with restrictions
nothing builds character
better than facing the fantasy
of love
and coming away
clean
the dream runs deep
deep as madness
unnatural as ocean waves
losing their want of the shore

press play rewind and play again

THEN

all the years of stuffed down emotions suddenly
come bubbling up – volcanic explosions tears and
anger and laughter – all the hundreds of times you
never said it and wanted to, fear, now pouring
forth lava-like everywhere – funny thing – you
don't care, this release is like nothing – no drug,
no magazine ad induced confusion convincing
you of what you are not, waking up and realizing
you are – you really are. you are truth – and dare
– you have snakes and ladders inside you and
you – can go everywhere Go-d-aim-it. so you do.
and you choose south – where restless winds sing
– keep singing until your thoughts sync with it.
wind songs flying through your brain. clarity is
yours and there is no way you can ever go back.
you are aware. you have been touched. dust and
sunshine. your song is set and sent so sing loud the
sound inside you. sound that's been locked down
for so long – find your name inside it. sun-power
light. it is your birthright your purpose, will and
reason. you can't know more, not now you've been
touched by a tornado – so blow

Much Worse

black birds are talking
nonsense
a lot of gossip
and half truths
speaking in tongues
complaining
as we do

when things can be
much worse

who teaches the birds
to mock us?
follow us?
copy us?
and show us
how silly we are

when things can be
much worse

He Tangata, He Tangata, He Tangata (Life is People)

the highs are higher, here
the moon more silver
time takes on shapes
ripe fruit ready in the orchard
crossing over
through black voids
dying a shaman's death
to exist amongst men
with slapped red chests
black-lipped sisters
hymnal rhythmz
thick as natural syrup
healing the heart

decorative weapons
warriors of the mind
kind kin begin again
after disaster fallen heritage
delivering messages
to move on
fear not, move on

beautiful people
of bright song
you brown relations
strong people
of swelling pride
land and sea with territories
of brave wave travellers
teams with fierce intentions
stood before women
unwounded, unwavering
protection
tribal people of wood and reeds
feathers and ink mysteries
in genealogy
the wind, the wind, the wind
listen

blood wars
love chants
walking original canvas
storytellers, prophecies
grow and thrive
this era of interesting time
this area of airborne light
this place of honey magic
from the vigilant bumble bee
I love it

together we stand
in the sun
and cast new shadows
over welcoming grasses

I want to trace the silhouette
and dress the naked spaces
with words of appreciation
but there are no words I know
in any language
written or spoken
to define the depth of emotion
this movement
these memories
our time together
can describe

regretfully, I have nothing
nothing, but these inadequate expressions
to leave as a way to say
Life is People
Life is People
Life is People

The Memory of Me

I wait
for the rain
to wash away
emotional
displays

I see my heart
on the wall
unfinished unframed
swollen and ashamed

I welcome the dusk
misty-coloured light
tucked in tight
a healing sleep
long and deep
one day to awake
again

I speak my wishes
to listening winds
and step with faith
away from a shaky world

I lie flat across
an orange shore
and watch fires
light up dry riverbeds
I find my place
in another land

for now, wrap me in moist moss
and carry me to my burial
where I'll wait for the rain
to wash the memory
of me

Chasing 7's

there is nothing left to lose
and there is no more time
take all those perfumed
letters from the closet
review them
proof in words
that you were loved once
it's not urgency
not even emergency
you have prepared for this time
many times over
considered who would play
you in the movie and who
would write the book
the balance of this reality
hangs in the hope
of love, your survivors
will have their say
and life will go on
it won't be the cardiac attack
that takes you
but disconnect from heart-matters
you saw the world
as your personal candy-store
no more rock 'n roll
where you're going

left in your wake will be
those who'll mourn
and those who'll spit
every broken promise
every lie will appear
as Technicolor monsters
looking like insurmountable
mountains leading to the other side
no time at all for desperate
attempts to reconcile
the nickel's been played
the numbers are rolling
you're left waiting
for those 7's

What Did You Do Boy

morning passes   around sleep   through the
   room   dreams change   surface aggressive
      to meet the harsh glare of day   soon they
      will discover   the soft mound   they will
         examine the remains   they will wonder
   what took place   and the dreams   play it
expertly again   tossing winds   plotting the
escape   mid-day approaches   no more hours
of rest   the road waits   under an unforgiving
   sun   the road waits   its wise understanding
works in tandem   what have you done   what
      has just happened   who was that?   chase
wealth   forget yourself   discover the worst of
future possibilities   don't be late   the day tick-
tocks on   breaks through dream time   redirect
      fate   escape   escape   take time   fight
         heat   drive man   press ahead   zero to
         ninety   eighty-five degrees   no trees for
shade   press ahead   drive freedom   it didn't
      happen   did it?   it didn't happen   did
   it?   what if   where are the boys now?   the
      ones who trained and dedicated their lives to
this   where are the foot-soldiers?   free   they
         didn't do the do   miles pile up behind
   you   gas up   go   keep going   tomorrow
may not happen   morning is too many hours
      away   cities towns farm yards away   the
         road   opens like your lover's legs   my
god man   was there no other way   you let
emotions take hold   now look at you   running
   into nothing   nothing but a handful of cash
for comfort   you were fooled   that money is
   worthless   it can't buy you tomorrow   and
         the dirt mound   will stay silent for
      now   you drive   put miles between the
truth   drive   fast   along a freeway   a lonely
   road   rushing air pulling at thoughts   road
         kill   faster   manslaughter   faster
            forgive me father   faster   forget
   it   drive   faster   what did you do boy?
               what did you do?

Easy Time

sentences drop
like hammers on concrete
condemned   to live inside
the state doling out fate
blurring the space
between   wrongright

innocence
goes ignored
unproven truth
slips past intelligence
gets sold as   emotional   blackmail
to a jury called peers

easy time

accused are used to this
accustomed to
being mistreated
years of incarceration
will be easy
nothing new here

quiet ones
lie low reluctantly
choose sides
when they have to
secretly long for a genuine friend
silence and safety

alpha-boys
challenge and retreat
they beat the bars
and feign bravery
on the range
men, impressing men
they pretend
it doesn't hurt

inside – till the end
looking out at life
witnessing from afar
trials and tribulations we endure
while they do easy time

Unusual

the kids were spooked
they never said
what they saw
they never spoke
about it at all

old ones told us
"the worlds were over-lapping,
expect the unexpected – expect the unusual"

late at night, I listened
while the wind
raced through branches – over grasses
whistled and howled
a sort of song
absent of comfort
so unusual a sound

mad cats and pained voices competing

it transfixed me
pushed a message into me
it was saying
"evil finds ways to fit in"
drawing blood from my heart

I was shaking, and taken
to another world
where time has no place

I will not say what I saw

it was the song
in the wind
a sound so haunting
remains a nameless
silent burden, burned
as unkind memories
to be forgotten

Sparkle

pots boil over
lucky bits of moisture escape
torture singe red elements
sounding like someone cooking drugs
down the hall in a vacant room
between trips back to reality
and you

my spirit is quiet
in its fleshy shell
where it feeds on
ego
desire
inspiration
mistakes
the fairies wait
to make magical acts of temptation
and dot my path with danger

the ambulance wails in pain
distracts nature
and natural acts of beauty
telling us
accidents are never accidents
rarely are they what they seem to be

rivers keep running
thick with fish
nature takes its cruel course
while acts of euthanasia are conducted
daily spitting on the masterpiece
spreading feces in the kingdom
rushing in…rushing out
the memory barely having time
to take shape

fear and love are bound together
in similar lessons
rocks live in water-filled pails
left out under the sun

they sparkle in moisture
so like torture, that's where
they live distressed

everything sparkles

Boiling Flesh

water moves
in rolling boil
ready for flesh
tidbits for appetites
we delight
in our suffering
and turn away
from the mundane

learn to push
our dreams
to the side
ignoring the challenge
to recall
our true selves
the burden of authenticity
takes us
from comfort
to flexibility
uncertainty
constant questioning

do we dance
in our own skin
or take our place
in another light
to reveal all
that makes our mouths water
boiling rolling
ready for flesh
to touch the tongue

we've come
too far to pass
our power to others
let them tell us
we are aboriginal
I must have missed that memo
we've yet to discover
the purpose of our suffering
instead, wait for payday
and blow it all
in one

Women's Work

the bounty of earth teaches us
obedience
we know what to do in changing seasons
the earth moves with us
surviving fierce summers

respectful relations
yield self-determined nations

clans co-habit collectively
politics and management
overseen by the mothers
listening to grandmothers
who sit and watch the earth turn

we learn
there is only good
and twisted versions of good
separate from things
that bring us closer to identities
of who we are   not
out of balance with natural rhythms
having to grasp at unsure answers

realizing your connection
to your national identity
has nothing to do with "canadian"
their short-comings will be
forgiven but never forget
the apology or adoption

we share a good soup
and gather in good health

women relay lessons given
through supernatural communications
to reunite a troubled couple
calm expectant mothers
teach the children with patience
and instruct the men
who can rule

All Fours

pure moments can be measured
by thimbles
and there ain't many of those, at that
do we not know
the country is an illusion
and when we pledge allegiance
it is all in vain
like root root rooting for the home team
we look in shallow graves
under rocks
and inside the mouths of babes
for anything we can trust
anything can save
cum inside
trust me

I'd rather sell my soul
for a rocket ship ride
than waste my time
my finite man-made hours
of work and toil
for something as conventional
as family
for anything as conditional
as love
have your tickets ready everybody
this train is about to leave the station

penetration always costs
costs someone in the end
my people
and when I say my people
I mean – me
know how to bend, beg and pretend
for gold
and when I say gold
I mean – crumbs
abundance – saves
generosity – delivers
words – lie

literacy is an overrated liberty
it teaches us to forget
don't write it down
don't repeat it
I want wings
I want to return
I want
and when I say I
I mean – You
I mean your eyes and mouth and hands
hold on – cowboy
have it your way
have it – and hand it over
let me see that gold tooth

"fight ya for it"

I Have Not Forgotten

ask hard questions
wonder why
I continue to play along
and search daily
for answers that feel right inside

when the sun sinks
I change
my reasons to care
disappear behind horizons
and in the dark
it becomes clear

what matters
is all relative
to everything else
its no secret we are all
related, codependant, in a symbiotic existence

while connections are stretched
in all directions at once
is it destiny we'll see?
what's next?

tell me – you know – what i want to hear
i'll dance in my resolve
to believe you
suspend my reality
just to make it true

at night
chaos increases
our breathing eases
eagles begin to feed
can you hear them
screech and mate
funny, it all sounds the same

Urges

immediate gratification
like seeing in 3-D
from all four directions
including top, bottom and inside

vapour's virtuous
time temptress
working to deadline every time
making crazy and inviting
everybody into the boat

we know
from our own definition of sanity
and our own levels of
acceptance
that danger is a tight-rope walk
being given the gift to see
beyond
to live quite comfortably
apart from
while others fear silence
and non-acceptance

fear of the unknown
is what drives these gifts to their heights
bleeds me of conditioning
and convention
roll and keep rolling for days
past the preconceived destination
travelling in complete darkness
towards...who knows

I heard the French poets
and liked the way their tongues
twisted the words, licked the syllables
and seduced me phrase by phrase
without translation

I heard the Cree speakers
spit the language

newly learned and worked
into fantastic poetry
brilliant, clever verses
so masterfully delivered

I heard the young poets sounding like
every other poet suffering from
cardiac arrest, detesting the sameness
in their breath and verse
cynically thinking to myself
it's all right, you'll grow out of it

I didn't listen
to the voices telling me to tame
it down and slow up the pace
I turned off the noise
but kept the rhythms going
because being interesting
is the goal
not entertaining, I'm not a clown
but a chef of literary goodness
cooking up plates of word food
something for you to say
I'm full and yet left wanting
more

morning is sacred
for in it clarity lives
and many times we race past
the hours when everything is
stripped down to perfection
but we can save it
for more daylight
brighter times
more powerful truth
knocking at the door
asking to come in

the patterns of this land
are not built on roads

it holds many paths
pick one
and follow it to the end
for once
never stray off course
because commitment
is its own reward
and truth really does set us free
freedom is never done with us
no one can give it
no one can take it away

Did Ya Feel it?

did you have to take
all the magic
leaving a deep void
like wind racing through tunnels
or a black starless night sky
winning was warm and pink
relaxed
anxiety wrapped in accomplishments
that put anger and rage to rest

I used to shake with thunder
in my sides, the memory of it
still makes me smile
love
served us well for a time
brief and full of relief
believing in itself through us
it tingled on my skin
like sun-kisses
citrus sensations kept us
coming back for more

inside and out
the lies and doubt
sat like stones in the stomach
biting noises in my head
unity confused
and soon
all was lost
forced to find solace in
strange ways, among strangers
every day a different mask
red then blue then black
spirit and truth can't find me
to this day

how do you feel?

(T)here is a Time

guess it will always be
the place of swollen
spring rivers
drowned brown currents
bursting through
breaking picket lines

the place where land clans
stand together .
muddied resolutions
cop confusion
scratch the surface
get a racist

the Grand place
that drank my dad's ashes
fed him and led him
roll'n, down the river
where he introduced us to soup
and *scon*
he's gone, but his skin
lives on, in me

it'll always be the last place
my niece and me was seen
barely connected, disconnected
by a thin film of colonial displacement
before her slippery trip
back into the big sleep
recounting our visit with
E. Pauline our rip roar'n ride
down 6th Line smoke shack, after
smoke shack, after smoke dance
after smoke shack
that time (t)here

here I'm a transplanted import
West Coast Mohawk
on Coast Salish Territory
this cedar place, my P.O.B.

where words found me
and took root
wind – ocean – forest – mountains

the land of
Great Big Red Skins
Old Growth origins
never removed
or broken traditions
but boarding school torture
and plenty of it
still lingers among
descendants knowing nothing
else but this
really real reality

I am in love
and vowed out loud
to one day die here
for I, too, won't feel this body
or have need of the land
while ascending to heavens
past rivers
not mine but theirs
not theirs but there/here
where does it all live

in the pages of map books
in memories
how does it look
the same as when they first came
to me, it is salmon candy
death defying drives
passing through
not passing through
occupied
in-habit
a-dopting
adapting
adjusting

accepting
yes, I'm accepted
not as one of theirs
I'll always be
the independent hi-bred bird
flown here from over (t)here

Acknowledgements

My greatest heartfelt thank you I extend to my
mother. I was born to my friend and friends we
will forever remain. I am grateful for the expert
editing by Garry Gottfriedson; a wise man, a great
poet and generous collaborator. With his help this
collection was elevated to eloquent oratory. I raise
my hands in thanks to the traditional land of the
Coast Salish people on whose territory I have been
a fortunate visitor for the last seventeen years.
This land is the inspiration for much of the poetry
found in these pages.

Last, but not least, I acknowledge the good work
Ursula Vaira does through Leaf Press. Ursula
produces jewels of literature and I am honoured to
have my words and messages live within her label.

About the Author

Janet is a Mohawk/Tuscarora writer from the Six Nations band in southern Ontario. She was born in Vancouver, British Columbia, and has been living on the traditional lands of the Coast Salish people (Victoria, British Columbia) since 1994. Janet works in the genres of poetry, short fiction, science fiction, play writing, spoken-word performance poetry, video poetry and recorded poems with music.

Her first published collection of poems is titled *Splitting the Heart* (Ekstasis Editions, 2007), which contains a companion CD of the same name. Janet has collaborated with musicians as a lyricist and has read with dance troupes, creating unique segments of mixed media presentations.

Janet's second video poem was launched in October 2009 and titled *What Did You Do Boy* in support of a spoken-word track from her CD *Firewater,* which earned nominations at the Canadian Aboriginal Music Awards 2009 and the Native American Music Awards 2010.

You can hear Janet on the air waves hosting *Native Waves Radio,* Vancouver Island's only native radio program, on CFUV 101.9 FM in Victoria; and "Tribal Clefs," a native music column, on CBC Radio One's program *All Points West* in British Columbia.

Ojistah Publishing (Mohawk word for star) is Janet's publishing label from which *Red Erotic,* a collection of indigenous erotic poetry and artwork was released in November 2010.